The MAILBOX®

grade 1

Prompt, Plan, Write.

D1318678

Practice for **FIVE** types of writing...

- Story writing
- Personal narratives
- Descriptive writing
- Friendly letters
- Simple instructions

Written by Catherine Broome-Kehm

Managing Editor: Gerri Primak

Editorial Team: Becky S. Andrews, Kimberley Bruck, Sharon Murphy, Debra Liverman, Diane Badden, Thad H. McLaurin, Lynn Drolet, Karen A. Brudnak, Jennifer Nunn, Hope Rodgers, Dorothy C. McKinney

Production Team: Lori Z. Henry, Pam Crane, Rebecca Saunders, Chris Curry, Sarah Foreman, Theresa Lewis Goode, Greg D. Rieves, Eliseo De Jesus Santos II, Barry Slate, Donna K. Teal, Zane Williard, Tazmen Carlisle, Kathy Coop, Marsha Heim, Lynette Dickerson, Mark Rainey, Karen Brewer Grossman, Laurel Robinson

76 Reproducible Writing Activities

www.themailbox.com

Table of Contents

What's Inside

76 REPRODUCIBLE WRITING ACTIVITIES...

for independent work, center work, small-group work, and homework!

ENGAGING PROMPT

SKILL LINE SHOWING THE TYPE OF WRITING

PREWRITING ORGANIZER TO HELP STUDENTS PLAN

WRITING TASK

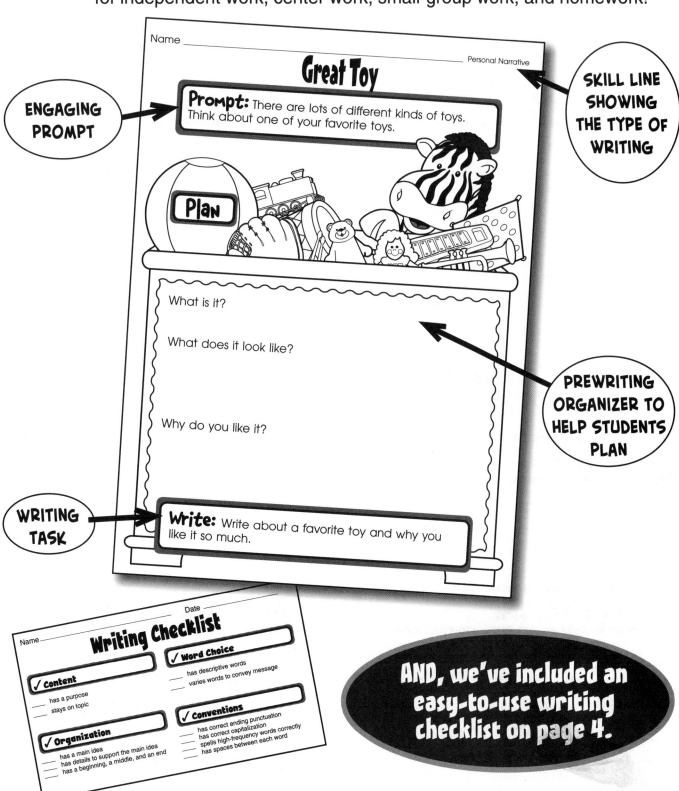

Name _____

Personal Narrative

Great Toy

Prompt: There are lots of different kinds of toys. Think about one of your favorite toys.

Plan

What is it?

What does it look like?

Why do you like it?

Write: Write about a favorite toy and why you like it so much.

Date _____

Writing Checklist

Name _____

✓ **Content**
___ has a purpose
___ stays on topic

✓ **Organization**
___ has a main idea
___ has details to support the main idea
___ has a beginning, a middle, and an end

✓ **Word Choice**
___ has descriptive words
___ varies words to convey message

✓ **Conventions**
___ has correct ending punctuation
___ has correct capitalization
___ spells high-frequency words correctly
___ has spaces between each word

AND, we've included an easy-to-use writing checklist on page 4.

3

Name _____ Date _____

Writing Checklist

✓ Content

_____ has a purpose

_____ stays on topic

✓ Organization

_____ has a main idea

_____ has details to support the main idea

_____ has a beginning, a middle, and an end

✓ Word Choice

_____ has descriptive words

_____ varies words to convey message

✓ Conventions

_____ has correct ending punctuation

_____ has correct capitalization

_____ spells high-frequency words correctly

_____ has spaces between each word

©The Mailbox® • *Prompt, Plan, Write!* • TEC61103

- -

Name _____ Date _____

Writing Checklist

✓ Content

_____ has a purpose

_____ stays on topic

✓ Organization

_____ has a main idea

_____ has details to support the main idea

_____ has a beginning, a middle, and an end

✓ Word Choice

_____ has descriptive words

_____ varies words to convey message

✓ Conventions

_____ has correct ending punctuation

_____ has correct capitalization

_____ spells high-frequency words correctly

_____ has spaces between each word

©The Mailbox® • *Prompt, Plan, Write!* • TEC61103

Healthful Treats

Prompt: Monkey is hungry. She is going to buy some fresh fruit to make a snack.

Plan

What fruit does Monkey buy?	What will she make with her fruit?

Write: Write a story that tells about the fruit Monkey bought and what she did with it.

Sleeping Bag Buddies

Prompt: Bear asked two friends to his sleepover.

Plan

Bear

Draw the two friends and write their names.

Write: Write a story about Bear's sleepover with his friends.

Name _____

Vet Visit

Prompt: Poor Foxy! He had to go to the vet.

Plan

What is wrong with Foxy?

Write: Write a story about Foxy's visit to the vet.

Lunchbox Surprise

Prompt: Bunny was very surprised when she opened her lunchbox!

Plan

What was Bunny's surprise?	Did she like her surprise?

Write: Write a story about Bunny's lunchbox surprise. Tell why she did or did not like the surprise.

Name

Catch of the Day

Prompt: It is an exciting day of fishing at the pond for Ron and Ricky!

Plan

What did Ron catch?

What did Ricky catch?

Write: Write a story about what Ron and Ricky caught during their day at the pond.

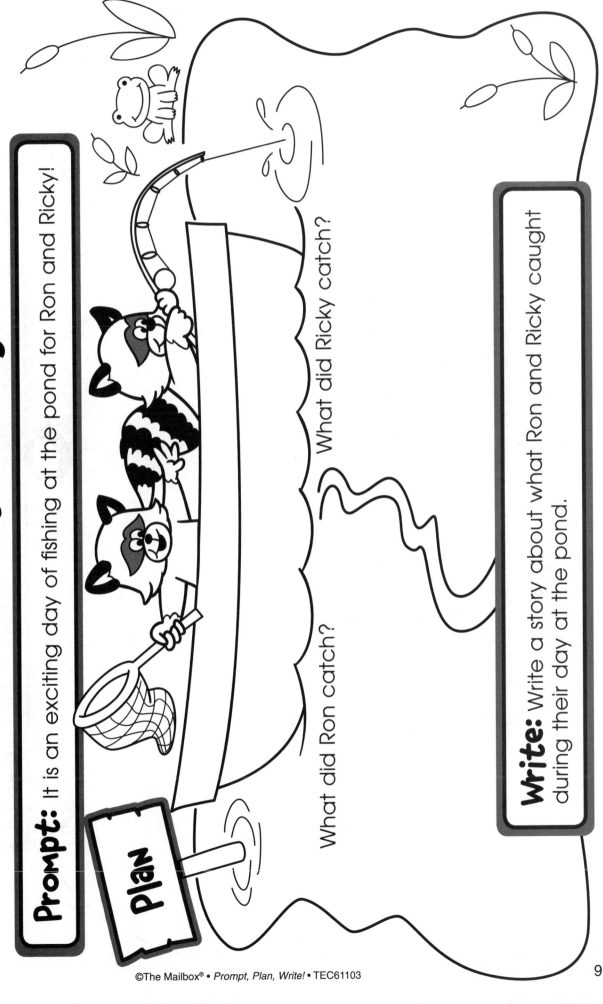

9

Pleasing the Twins

Prompt: Panda is baby-sitting twins. The babies are not very happy.

Plan

Why are the twins crying?

What will Panda do to help the twins stop crying?

Write: Write a story that tells why the twins are crying and what Panda does to solve the problem.

Hiccup Help

Prompt: Hippo started to hiccup while reading to the class. What two things can she do to get rid of her hiccups?

Hiccup

① ② Plan

Write: Write a story that tells how Hippo got her hiccups to stop.

Name _____

Morning Exercises

Prompt: Kangaroo is getting ready for his workout.

What are some exercises Kangaroo can do?

Plan

Write: Write a story that tells about the exercises Kangaroo does during his workout.

Name _____

In the Garden

Prompt: Mole works hard to help her garden grow.

What work does Mole do in the garden?

Plan

What is she growing?

Write: Write a story that tells about Mole's garden and the work that she does to help it grow.

©The Mailbox® • *Prompt, Plan, Write!* • TEC61103

Name _____

Cave Discovery

Prompt: Turtle is very curious. He decides to explore a dark cave.

What does he do after he finds it?

What does Turtle find inside the cave?

Plan

Write: Write a story about what happens when Turtle explores a dark cave. Be sure to tell what he finds and what he does after he finds it.

Name _____

Seeing the Sights

Prompt: Sheep likes to fly his plane in the sky. He sees many things as he travels.

What are two things Sheep sees as he flies his plane?

Plan

①

②

Write: Write a story that tells about what Sheep sees while he flies his plane.

That Is Funny!

Prompt: Clara Clown is silly. She likes to make people laugh.

Plan

What two things will Clara do to make people laugh?

①

②

Write: Write a story that tells how Clara makes people laugh.

Barn Bash

Prompt: The barn animals are having a party.

Plan

Who is at the party?

Why are they having a party?

What are they doing at the party?

Write: Write a story that tells about the barn animals' party.

Lost and Found!

Prompt: Owl lost her glasses! In what three places will she look for them?

Plan

①

②

③

Write: Write a story about Owl's search for her glasses. Be sure to tell about where she looked and where the glasses were found.

Amazing Bugs

Prompt: Froggy sees some amazing bugs! He wants to get a closer look!

Plan

How does Froggy get the bugs into the jar?

What is amazing about the bugs?

Write: Write a story about how Froggy got some amazing bugs into a jar.

A Shared Meal

Prompt: Pig is making dinner for some friends. She made a tasty soup to share with them.

Plan

Who are the friends Pig invited?

How does Pig know whether her friends like the soup?

Write: Write a story about Pig's dinner and the soup she shared with her friends.

Special Delivery

Prompt: A big box was delivered to your house. It's for you!

Who sent the box?	Why was it sent?

What is inside the box?	How do you feel about what was sent?

Write: Write a story about the special delivery. Be sure to share how you felt throughout the story.

Underwater View

Prompt: You are invited to take a submarine ride!

Plan

What do you see?

First

Second

Third

Write: Write a story about what you saw on your submarine ride.

Beach-Bound

Prompt: It is a hot day. Sandy has big plans for a fun day at the beach.

Plan

What will Sandy do?

First

Next

Last

Write: Write a story about Sandy's fun day at the beach.

Family Day

Prompt: It's Family Day, and you get to choose the events of the day!

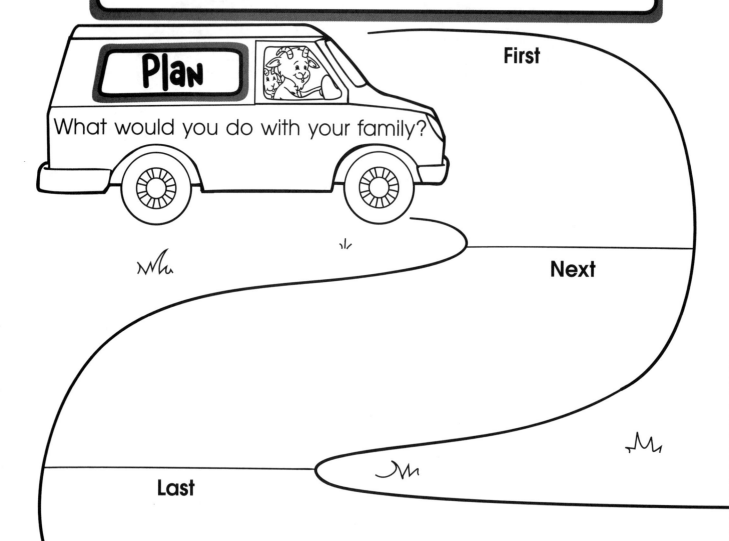

Plan

What would you do with your family?

First

Next

Last

Write: Write a story about what you would do with your family on Family Day.

Name _____

It's Show Time!

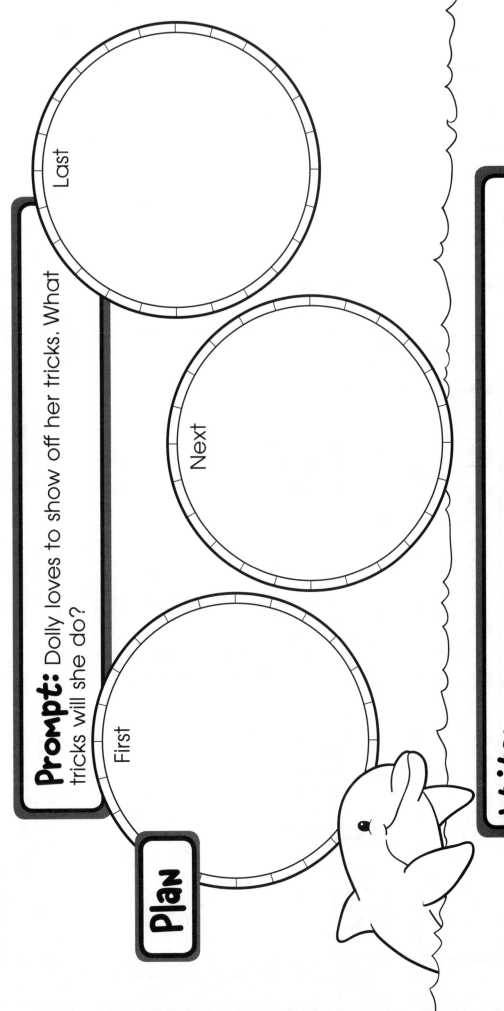

Prompt: Dolly loves to show off her tricks. What tricks will she do?

Last

Next

First

Plan

Write: Write a story about Dolly's tricks. Be sure to use the words **first**, **next**, and **last** in your writing.

Fun With Paint

Prompt: The kittens had a fun day after they found some paint! What happened?

Plan

Beginning

Middle

End

Write: Write a story about the kittens' day with the paint.

Tree Fort Fun

Prompt: The squirrels are spending the day in their new tree fort! What will they do?

Beginning

Middle

End

Write: Write a story about what the squirrels did when they spent the day in their new tree fort.

Backpack Surprise

Prompt: After visiting the zoo, you find a cuddly koala in your backpack! What will you do?

Plan   Beginning

Middle

End

Write: Write a story about finding a koala in your backpack. Tell what you did with it.

Pony's Adventure

Prompt: The gate was left open and Pony got away from the farm. What will she do?

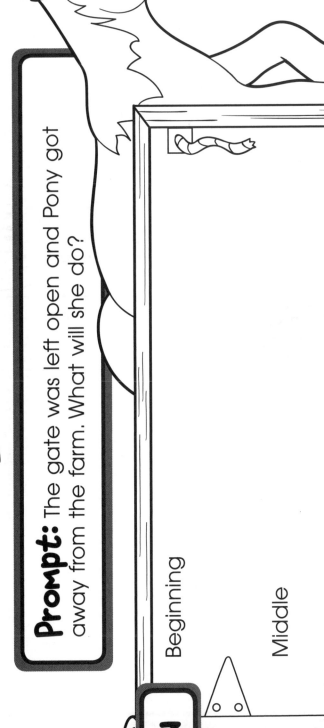

Plan

Beginning

Middle

End

Write: Write a story about Pony's day of adventure when the gate was left open.

A Great School Day

Prompt: Think about a really great day you had at school.

Plan

What made your day so great?

Write: Write about what happened during a really great day at school.

Name _____

A Great Trip

Prompt: Think about a fun trip you took.

Plan

Where did you go?

What did you do?

Write: Write about a fun trip. Be sure to tell where you went and what you did.

Helping Hand

Prompt: Think about a time when you helped someone.

Plan

What person did you help?

What did you do?

How did you feel after helping?

Write: Write about a time when you helped someone. Be sure to give details about what you did and how it made you feel.

A Quiet Place

Prompt: Think about a place you went to for some quiet time.

Plan

Why did you need quiet time?

Where did you go?

What did you do when you got there?

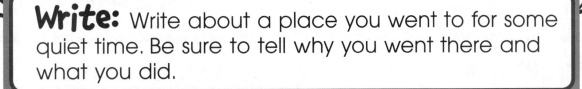

Write: Write about a place you went to for some quiet time. Be sure to tell why you went there and what you did.

Rainy Day

Prompt: Think about a recent rainy day. What are two things you like to do on a rainy day?

Plan

①   ②

Write: Write about the things you like to do on a rainy day.

Shopping Spree

Prompt: Think about a time you went to the store and saw something you really wanted.

Plan

What did you really want to get?

Why did you want it?

Did you get it? Why or why not?

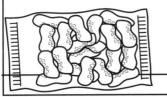

Write: Write about something you really wanted to get at the store. Be sure to tell why you wanted it and whether you got it.

Summer Fun

Prompt: Summer can be fun! Think about a fun day you had in the summer.

Plan

What are some things you did on the summer day?

Write: Write about the things you did on the fun summer day.

Name _____

Playing It Safe

Prompt: Think about how you play at the playground. What are some things that you do to stay safe?

Plan

Write: Write about the ways that you play safe at the playground.

Happy Birthday!

Prompt: Birthday parties can be fun. Think about a time you went to a birthday party.

Plan

Whose birthday party was it?

Who was there?

What did you do?

Write: Write about the things you did at the birthday party. Be sure to tell whom the party was for and who else was there.

Name _____

My Friends

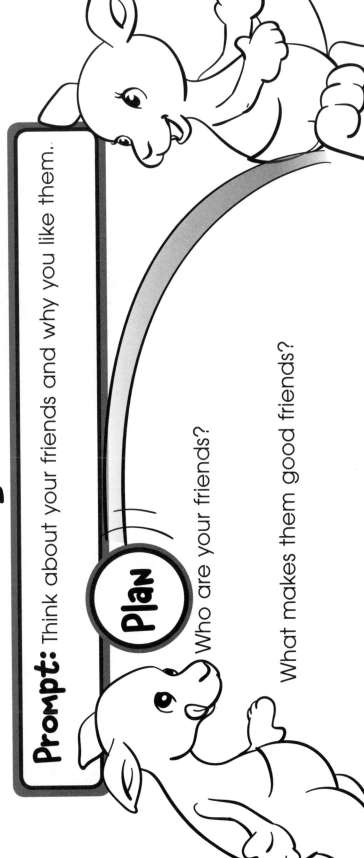

Prompt: Think about your friends and why you like them.

Plan

Who are your friends?

What makes them good friends?

Write: Write about your good friends and why you like them.

Favorite Games

Prompt: Games are fun to play! Think about a game you like to play.

Plan

What game do you like to play?

Who do you play it with?

Write: Write about the game you like to play and who plays it with you.

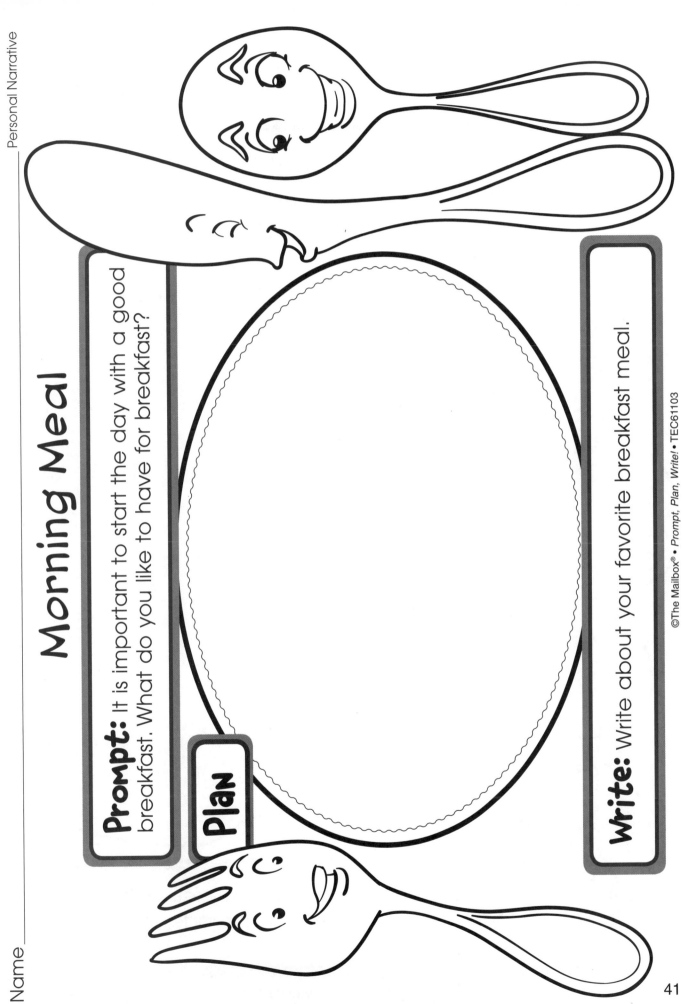

Name _____

Morning Meal

Prompt: It is important to start the day with a good breakfast. What do you like to have for breakfast?

Plan

Write: Write about your favorite breakfast meal.

©The Mailbox® • *Prompt, Plan, Write!* • TEC61103

Feeling Lucky

Prompt: Think about a day when you felt lucky.

Plan

What are some things that happened that made you feel lucky?

Write: Write about a day when you felt lucky. Be sure to tell about the things that made you feel that way.

Terrific Talent

Prompt: Think about something you are really good at doing.

Plan

What do you do well?

When do you do it?

Write: Write about something you are really good at doing and when you do it.

It's Homemade

Prompt: Homemade things are special. Think about something you like to make.

Plan

What do you like to make?	Why do you like to make it?

Write: Write about something you like to make and tell why you like to make it.

Teamwork

Prompt: Think about a time when you worked with others to get something done.

Plan

What did you do?

Who helped you?

Write: Write about a time when you worked with others to get something done. Be sure to share what the job was and who helped.

Impressive!

Prompt: Think about a time when you felt very proud of yourself.

What did you do that made you feel proud?

Who else was proud of you?

Write: Write about a time when you and others were proud of something you did.

Lost Tooth

Prompt: Some kids lose baby teeth in first grade. Think of a day when you lost a tooth.

Plan

Where were you when you lost the tooth?

What did you do with the tooth?

Write: Write about a day when you lost a tooth. Be sure to tell where you were and what you did with it.

Outside Fun

Prompt: Enjoying the outdoors on a nice day can be fun. What are three things you like to do outside on a nice day?

Plan

1
2
3

Write: Write about the things you like to do outside on a nice day.

Ouch!

Prompt: It's nice to have someone help you if you get hurt. Think about a time when you got hurt.

Plan

How did you get hurt?

Who helped you?

Write: Write about a time when you got hurt and who helped you.

My Favorite Season

Prompt: There are lots of things to do during each of the four seasons. Think about which season you like the most.

Plan

winter

spring

Which season is your favorite?

What do you like about the weather?

What things do you like to do?

summer

fall

Write: Write about your favorite season. Be sure to give details telling why it is your favorite.

Name _____

Cute As Can Be

Prompt: Think about one of the cutest things you have ever seen.

What was it?

What did it look like?

Where did you see it?

Plan

Write: Write about one of the cutest things you have ever seen. Be sure to describe it and tell where you saw it.

©The Mailbox® • *Prompt, Plan, Write!* • TEC61103

51

Wishful Thinking

Prompt: Wishes sometimes can come true! Think about a time you made a wish.

Plan

What did you wish for?

Why did you make the wish?

Did your wish come true?

Write: Write about what you wished for, why you made a wish, and whether it came true.

First Lesson

Prompt: Think about a time when someone taught you something new.

Plan

Who taught you?

What did you learn?

Are you still learning it?

Write: Write about a time when you learned something new. Be sure to tell who taught you and whether you are still learning it.

Great Toy

Prompt: There are lots of different kinds of toys. Think about one of your favorite toys.

Plan

What is it?

What does it look like?

Why do you like it?

Write: Write about a favorite toy and why you like it so much.

Name _____

My Teacher

Prompt: A writer from the newspaper wants to write about your teacher. She has asked you to describe your teacher.

Plan

Draw a picture of your teacher.

What are two things that you like best about your teacher?

_____

Write: Describe your teacher. Be sure to add lots of details.

©The Mailbox® • *Prompt, Plan, Write!* • TEC61103

Delicious Dessert

Prompt: Your favorite dessert has just been served.

Plan

What is it?

What does it look like?

What does it taste like?

Write: Describe your favorite dessert. Be sure to add details that tell why you like it so much.

Invent a Toy

Prompt: You have been asked to design a new toy.

Plan

What is the new toy?

What does the toy look like?

What does it do?

Write: Describe the new toy. Be sure to add details to your writing.

Silly Haircut

Prompt: Lion got a silly haircut!

Draw Lion's hair.

Plan

What makes the haircut look silly?

Write: Describe Lion's silly new haircut.

Descriptive Writing

Learning to Fly

Prompt: Pretend you are a baby bird learning to fly.

Plan

How do you feel?

What makes it easy or hard?

Write: Describe what it would be like to be a baby bird learning to fly. Be creative.

©The Mailbox® • *Prompt, Plan, Write!* • TEC61103

Snow Day

Prompt: Imagine you just woke up and there is five feet of snow on the ground.

What does it look like outside?

How does the snow feel?

What else describes the snowy morning?

Plan

Write: Describe the snowy scene that you see. Be sure to include lots of details.

©The Mailbox® • *Prompt, Plan, Write!* • TEC61103

Name

What a Game!

Prompt: Imagine you are at an exciting sporting event.

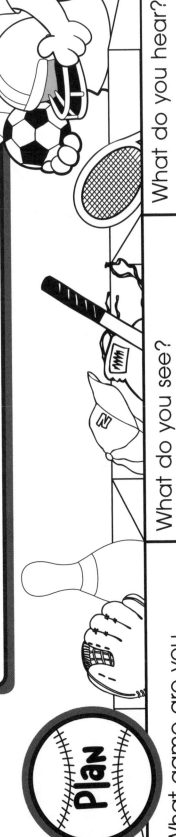

Plan

What game are you watching?

What do you see?

What do you hear?

Write: Describe the exciting sporting event. Be sure to add details.

Name _____

Beautiful Butterfly

Prompt: Imagine you just saw a butterfly fly by.

Plan

Draw the wings. Then color the butterfly.

List some words that describe the butterfly.

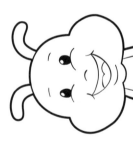
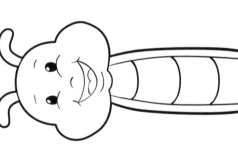

Write: Describe the butterfly. Be sure to use your list of words.

Name _____

Funny Dream

Prompt: While you were sleeping, you had a funny dream.

Plan

Describe two things that happened that made the dream funny.

Write: Describe your dream. Be sure to add details to tell what made it so funny.

I'm a Fish!

Prompt: Imagine you are a goldfish living in a fishbowl.

Plan

What is it like to be a fish?

What do you do in your home?

What do you see?

Write: Describe what it would be like to be a fish living in a fishbowl. Be sure to include details in your writing.

Train Delivery

Prompt: You see a train going by with loads of candy.

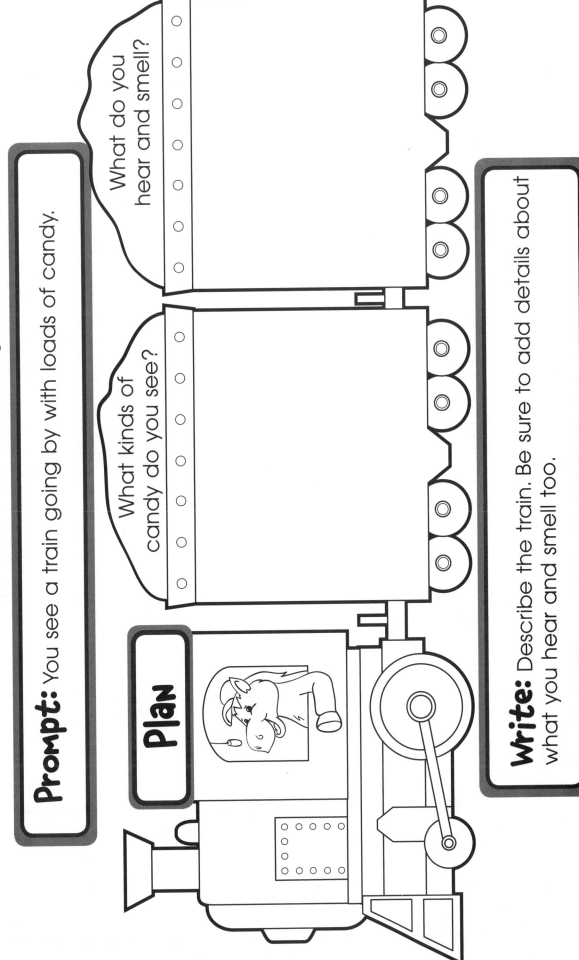

What do you hear and smell?

What kinds of candy do you see?

Plan

Write: Describe the train. Be sure to add details about what you hear and smell too.

©The Mailbox® • *Prompt, Plan, Write!* • TEC61103

A Special Friend

Prompt: You have been asked to make a display about your friend.

Plan

My Friend

_____
Draw your friend.

What are two things that remind you of your friend?

①

②

Write: Describe your friend. Be sure to use the display you made to give details about your friend.

I Want to Be a...

Prompt: Think about what you want to be when you grow up.

Plan

What will your job be?

What will you do at your job?

Give reasons for your job choice.

Write: Describe your future job and tell what you will do. Give details to explain why you want that kind of job.

Nice Place

Prompt: Think of a place you like to visit.

Where do you like to go?

Why do you like it there?

How does it smell?

What can you touch?

Write: Describe a place you like to visit and tell why you like to go there. Be sure to add details in your writing.

Space Visitor

Prompt: Imagine an alien just landed in your backyard.

Draw the alien.

Plan

What does it do to make you think that it is friendly or unfriendly?

Write: Describe the alien. Be sure to add details that tell whether you think the alien is friendly or not.

©The Mailbox® • *Prompt, Plan, Write!* • TEC61103

All About Me

Prompt: A new student named Cal will be in your class next week! Your teacher would like you to introduce yourself.

Plan

Write your name and age.

What are three things you want Cal to know about you?

Write: Write a letter to Cal telling him all about yourself.

Play Date

Prompt: It is Saturday, and you are allowed to invite a friend over to play!

Plan

What friend will you invite?

What will you do?

Write: Write a letter to a friend inviting him or her to play. Be sure to tell him or her what you will do.

©The Mailbox® • *Prompt, Plan, Write!* • TEC61103

A Super Teacher!

Prompt: You have entered your teacher in a contest to find the "World's Greatest Teacher."

Plan

What fun things does your teacher do?	What makes your teacher great?

Write: Write a letter to the judges. Tell them why your teacher should win the contest.

A Great Gift!

Prompt: Your friend just gave you the best gift!

Plan

Who gave you the gift?

What was the gift?

Why did he or she give you the gift?

Write: Write a letter to your friend. Thank him or her for the gift.

Building Plans

Prompt: You want Builder Billy to help you build a tree house.

Plan

Why do you want a tree house?

What will be special about your tree house?

Write: Write a letter to Builder Billy. Ask him to help you build the tree house. Be sure to tell him why you want the tree house and what will make it so special.

©The Mailbox® • *Prompt, Plan, Write!* • TEC61103

Muddy Buddy

Prompt: You are a pig named Buddy, and you love mud! The farmer wants to clean up all the mud on the farm.

Plan

Write two reasons why the farmer should not clean up the mud.

① _____

② _____

Write: Write a letter to the farmer. Tell him why he should not clean up the mud.

Lunch Bunch

Prompt: It is time for lunch! You want to make a peanut butter and jelly sandwich.

Plan

What things will you need?

Write: Write directions that tell how to make a peanut butter and jelly sandwich. Be sure to include everything you will need.

Wrapping Up

Prompt: Flo wants to wrap a gift for her mom. But she does not know how to wrap!

Plan

What does Flo need to wrap the gift?

Write: Write directions that tell Flo how to wrap the gift. Be sure to include everything she needs.

Splish Splash

Prompt: It's bathtime for Ducky!

Plan

What steps should Ducky follow to take a bath?

Write: Write directions to tell Ducky how to take a bath. Use words such as **first**, **second**, **third**, and **fourth** in your directions.

Growing Seeds

Prompt: You just bought a pack of flower seeds.

Plan

What steps do you need to follow to plant the seeds?

Write: Write directions to tell how to plant the seeds. Use words such as **first**, **next**, **then**, and **last** in your directions.

80 Name _____

Playing at the Park

Prompt: Going to the park is so much fun! Think about a favorite thing that you know how to do at the park.

Plan

I know how to

List the steps to tell how to do your favorite thing.

Write: Write directions that tell how to do your favorite thing at the park. Use words such as **first, next, then,** and **last** in your directions.